INSIDE THE
NFL

MINNESOTA
VIKINGS

BY TODD RYAN

SportsZone
An Imprint of Abdo Publishing
abdobooks.com

abdobooks.com

Published by Abdo Publishing, a division of ABDO, PO Box 398166, Minneapolis, Minnesota 55439. Copyright © 2020 by Abdo Consulting Group, Inc. International copyrights reserved in all countries. No part of this book may be reproduced in any form without written permission from the publisher. SportsZone™ is a trademark and logo of Abdo Publishing.

Printed in the United States of America, North Mankato, Minnesota
042019
092019

THIS BOOK CONTAINS RECYCLED MATERIALS

Cover Photo: Jeff Haynes/Panini/AP Images
Interior Photos: James Flores/Getty Images Sport/Getty Images, 5, 43; David Durochik/AP Images, 7; NFL Photos/AP Images, 9, 23; AP Images, 11, 13, 17, 20; Vernon Biever/AP Images, 15; JT/AP Images, 19; Jim Mone/AP Images, 25; Eric Risberg/AP Images, 27; Tom Olmscheid/AP Images, 29; Tim Sharp/AP Images, 31; David Stluka/AP Images, 35, 36; Greg Trott/AP Images, 38; David E. Klutho/Sports Illustrated/Set Number: X161626 TK1/Getty Images, 41

Editor: Patrick Donnelly
Series Designer: Craig Hinton

Library of Congress Control Number: 2018965654

Publisher's Cataloging-in-Publication Data

Names: Ryan, Todd, author.
Title: Minnesota Vikings / by Todd Ryan
Description: Minneapolis, Minnesota: Abdo Publishing, 2020 | Series: Inside the NFL | Includes online resources and index.
Identifiers: ISBN 9781532118562 (lib. bdg.) | ISBN 9781532172748 (ebook) | ISBN 9781644941102 (pbk.)
Subjects: LCSH: Minnesota Vikings (Football team)--Juvenile literature. | National Football League--Juvenile literature. | Football teams--Juvenile literature. | American football--Juvenile literature.
Classification: DDC 796.33264--dc23

TABLE OF CONTENTS

CHAPTER 1
PURPLE PEOPLE EATERS 4

CHAPTER 2
GROWING INTO GREATNESS 10

CHAPTER 3
CAN'T WIN THE BIG ONE 16

CHAPTER 4
GOING GREEN 24

CHAPTER 5
NEW ERA, SIMILAR RESULTS 34

TIMELINE	42
QUICK STATS	44
QUOTES AND ANECDOTES	45
GLOSSARY	46
MORE INFORMATION	47
ONLINE RESOURCES	47
INDEX	48
ABOUT THE AUTHOR	48

CHAPTER 1

PURPLE PEOPLE EATERS

Jim Marshall, Carl Eller, Alan Page, and Gary Larsen. They were the four men on the Minnesota Vikings' defensive line in the late 1960s and early 1970s. They were known as the Purple People Eaters, after a popular novelty song of the era.

Why? Because they wore purple uniforms and they swallowed up anyone carrying a football. The Purple People Eaters were among the most dominant defensive lines ever.

Marshall had been with the Vikings the longest. He came to Minnesota in the team's first season in 1961. Eller was added in 1964 and Larsen in 1965. Page came aboard in 1967. Their legend began to grow toward the end of the 1960s. When they gained experience playing together, they struck

Left to right, Jim Marshall, Carl Eller, Alan Page, and Gary Larsen were known as the Purple People Eaters.

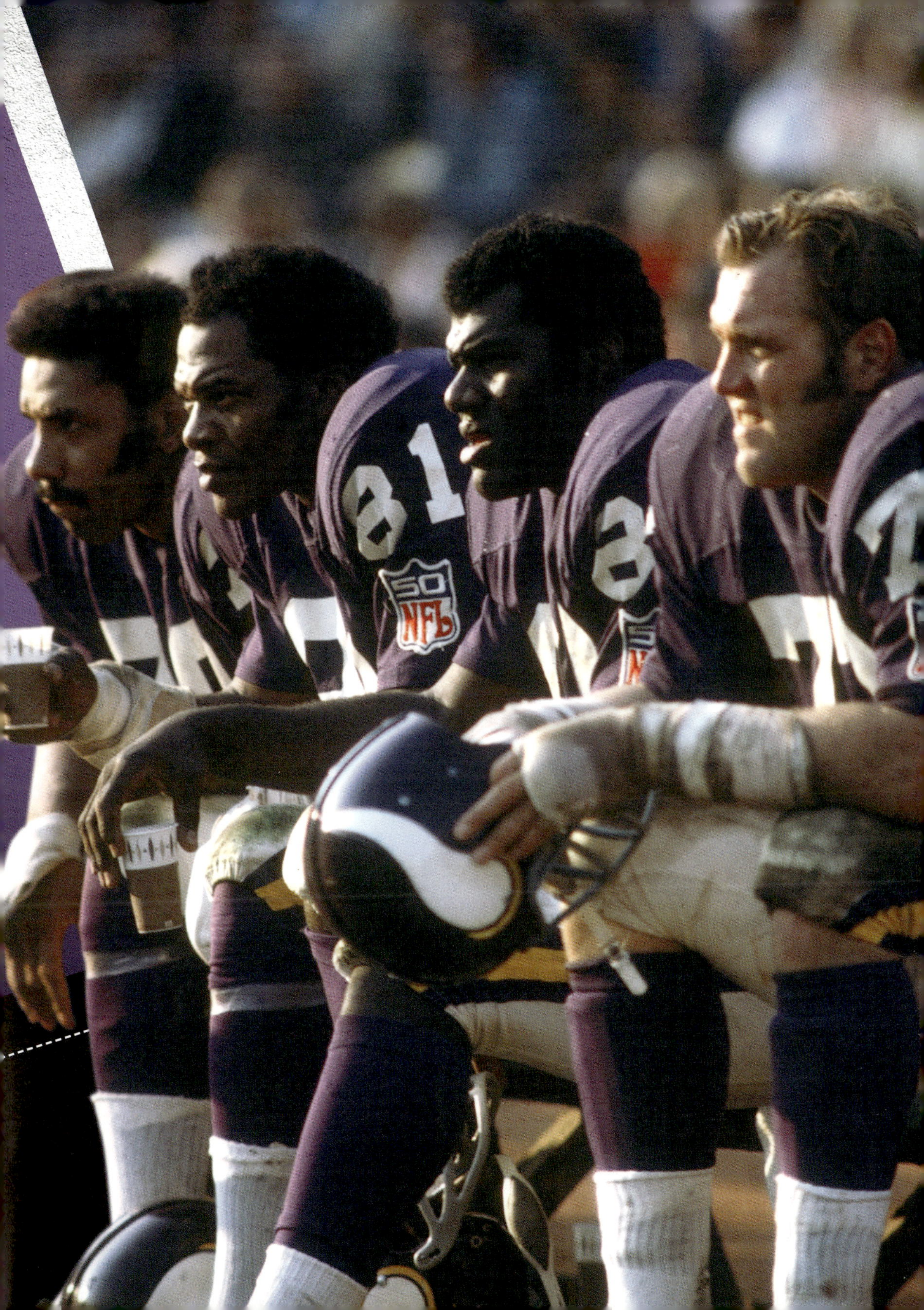
81
50
NFL

FROM THE FIELD TO THE BENCH

Athletes who wonder what they will do after they retire from sports can draw inspiration from former Vikings defensive lineman Alan Page.

Page recorded 173 sacks in his career. He was selected as the NFL Most Valuable Player (MVP) in 1971, a rare feat for a defensive player. But when he left the game, he did not merely look back at his achievements on the gridiron. He had already enrolled in law school at the University of Minnesota and passed his bar exam. He became so successful as a lawyer that he was elected to the Minnesota State Supreme Court in 1992.

Page retired from the bench in 2015. In 2018 he was named as one of seven recipients of the Presidential Medal of Freedom. Recipients are chosen by the President of the United States in recognition of their contributions to society. It is the highest award available to a civilian in the United States.

fear into running backs and quarterbacks throughout the National Football League (NFL).

The Vikings' defense blossomed in 1969. The Purple People Eaters were dominant, as usual. The secondary was becoming a force, too.

During their 14 regular-season games, the Vikings' defense allowed just 2,720 yards, 12 touchdowns, and 133 points. Opponents averaged only 9.5 points and fewer than 200 total yards per game. Minnesota surrendered 14 points or fewer in each of its final 13 regular-season games that season.

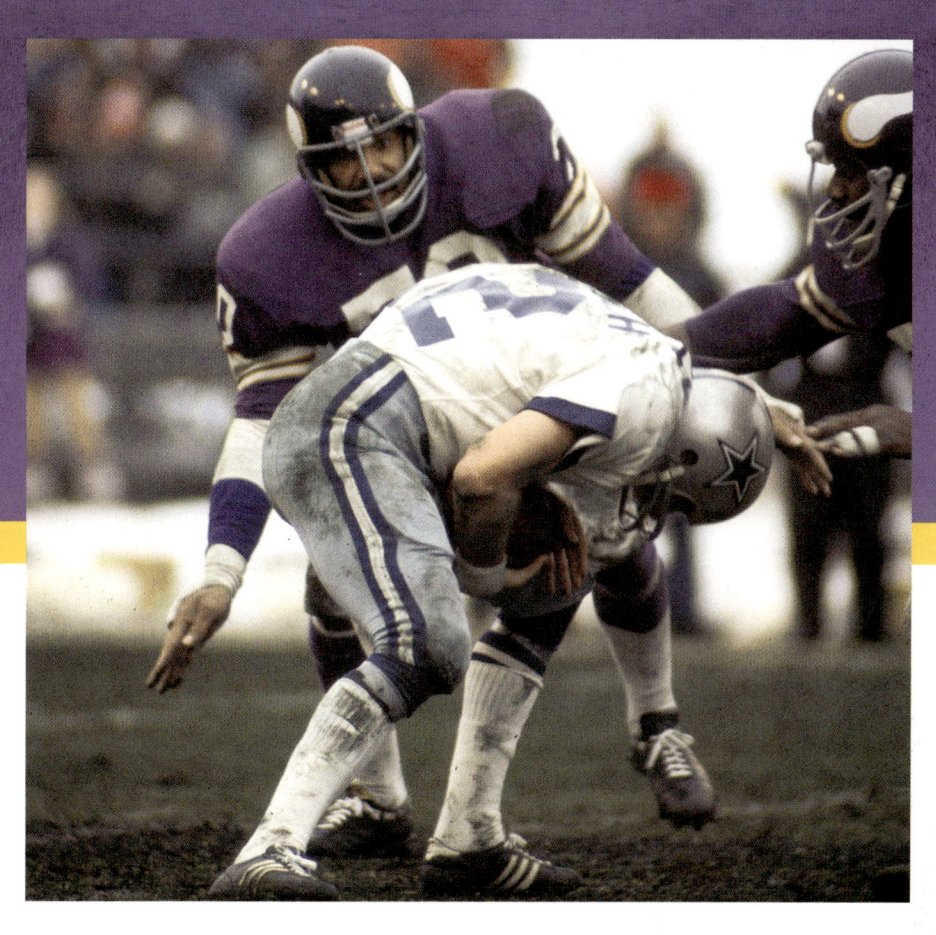

✕ Vikings defensive end Jim Marshall wraps up Cowboys quarterback Roger Staubach for a sack.

But it was not just the Vikings defense that stood out. Led by quarterback Joe Kapp, running back Dave Osborn, and wide receiver Gene Washington, Minnesota had one of the best offenses in the league, as well. The Vikings' offense compiled 4,096 yards and 39 touchdowns during the regular season. They led the NFL in scoring with 379 total points. Needless to say, the Vikings were tough to beat.

THE GREATEST THIEF OF ALL

The success of Vikings safety Paul Krause was often overshadowed by that of the Purple People Eaters. Krause is the NFL's career leader in interceptions with 81. He wasted no time establishing himself when he led the league with 12 as a rookie with Washington in 1964. He racked up at least five interceptions in nine of his first 12 years in the league. Krause was voted into eight Pro Bowls. He was enshrined in the Pro Football Hall of Fame in 1998.

The Vikings went 12–2 and won the NFL Central Division title. In the playoffs, they edged the visiting Los Angeles Rams 23–20 in the first round. It was the first playoff victory in team history. One week later they played host to the Cleveland Browns in the NFL Championship Game.

On January 4, 1970, with the temperature only 8 degrees Fahrenheit (minus-13°C), Minnesota dismantled the Browns. Kapp completed 7 of 13 passes for 169 yards and a touchdown. He rushed for another touchdown. Osborn carried the ball 18 times for 108 yards and a touchdown. Meanwhile, the Vikings' defense kept Cleveland's high-powered offense in check. The Vikings held a 27–0 lead late in the fourth quarter before the Browns finally scored a touchdown. It was not close to enough. Minnesota won 27–7.

Although the Vikings had won the NFL Championship Game, they still had one game to play. Starting in 1966, the NFL champion began playing the American Football League (AFL)

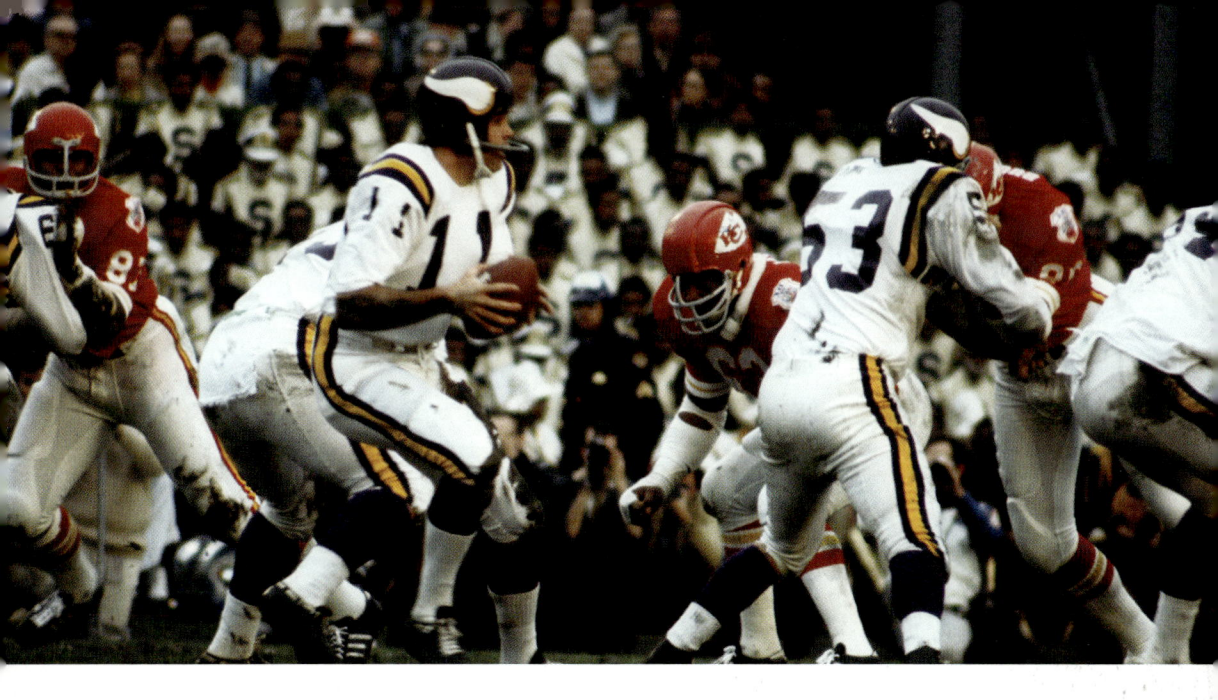

✗ **The Vikings' Joe Kapp drops back to pass against the Chiefs during Super Bowl IV. Kapp threw two interceptions in Minnesota's 23–7 loss.**

champion in the Super Bowl. In 1969 that was the Kansas City Chiefs, who would be Minnesota's opponent in Super Bowl IV.

The Vikings were expected to dominate the game. At the time, most observers still considered the NFL to be superior to the AFL. However, it was the other way around in Super Bowl IV.

As the Chiefs' offense slowly chipped away at the Purple People Eaters, Kansas City's defense completely shut down the Vikings' offense. Kapp threw two interceptions and the Vikings lost two fumbles. The underdog Chiefs cruised to a 23–7 win.

The Vikings had lost their first Super Bowl. Unfortunately for the team's fans, it was an experience that would soon become all too familiar.

CHAPTER 2

GROWING INTO GREATNESS

The birth of the Vikings occurred more than a year and a half before they stepped onto the field for their first game. Minnesota businessman Max Winter led a group that was originally slated to own one of the eight teams in the new AFL when that league began play in 1960. However, the NFL saw potential in the Upper Midwest, and on January 28, 1960, the league granted Winter's group the rights to own a franchise.

Among the first orders of business for the new team was to hire a head coach. They selected longtime NFL quarterback Norm Van Brocklin. Van Brocklin and general manager Bert Rose set out to stock the squad with the best players possible.

Minnesota quarterback Fran Tarkenton scrambles against the Green Bay Packers in 1966.

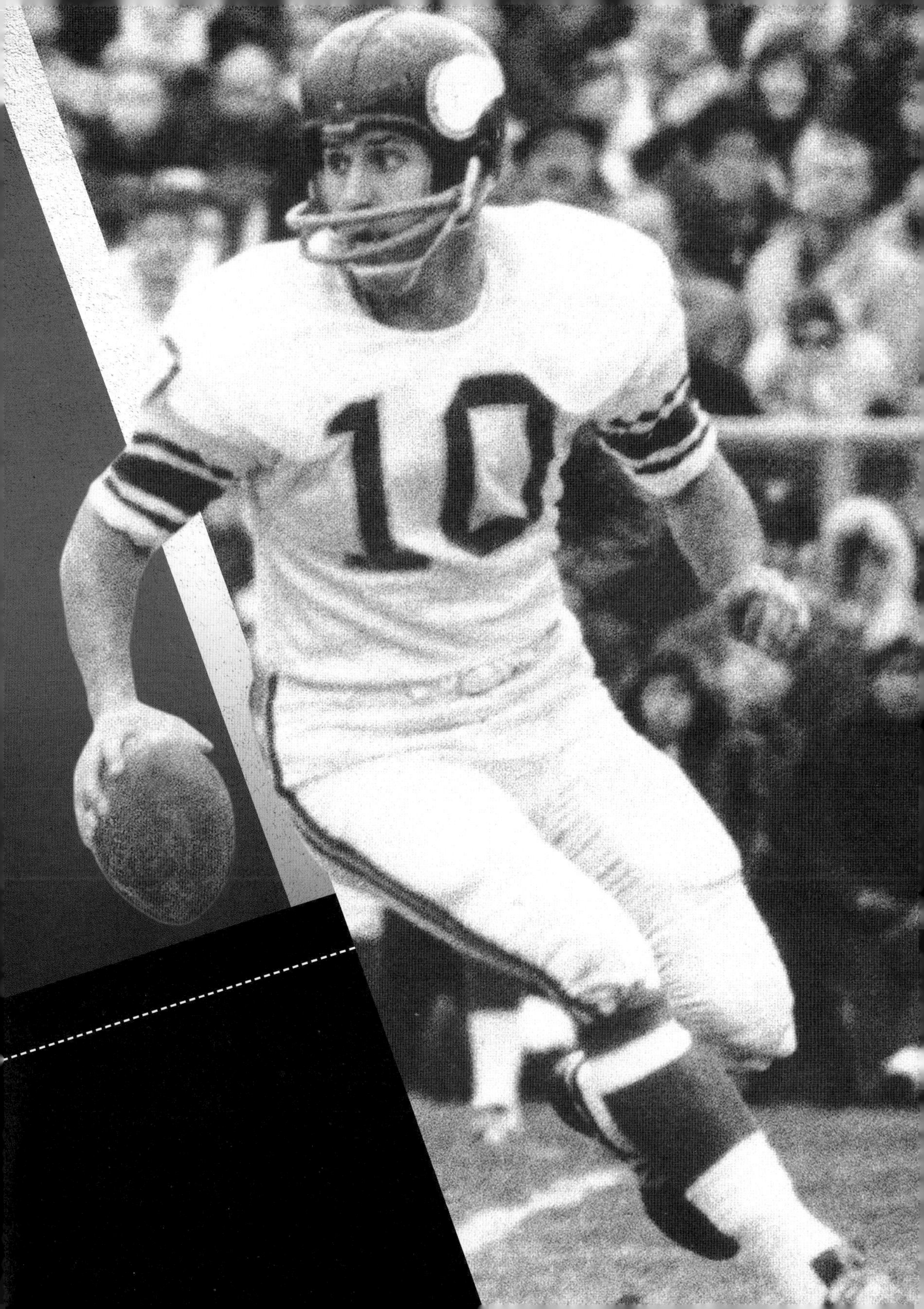
10

QB TO COACH

The Vikings apparently believed that Norm Van Brocklin needed no seasoning to be a head coach. He ended his career as a quarterback in 1960 by leading the Philadelphia Eagles to the NFL championship and winning the NFL MVP Award. Nine months later, he was guiding the Vikings from the sideline.

Van Brocklin had joined the Los Angeles Rams in 1949. He led the NFL in passing yards per attempt in 1950, 1951, 1952, and 1954. He threw for 554 yards in one game in 1951, a mind-blowing total that is still a league record. He also led the Rams to the title that year. Van Brocklin finished his career with 23,611 passing yards, 173 touchdown throws, and nine Pro Bowl appearances.

But he was far less successful as a coach. In six seasons in Minnesota, Van Brocklin never made the playoffs. He then coached the Atlanta Falcons for seven seasons with limited success. Van Brocklin was inducted into the Pro Football Hall of Fame in 1971.

The Vikings selected running back Tommy Mason and future Hall of Fame quarterback Fran Tarkenton in their first draft. They acquired talented players such as offensive lineman Grady Alderman, running back Hugh McElhenny, and wide receiver Jerry Reichow from other teams. They added center Mick Tingelhoff in 1962. By 1964, all of those players had represented the Vikings in the Pro Bowl.

Despite being a new team, the Vikings certainly came prepared to play in their very first game. The Chicago Bears were regular NFL title contenders under legendary coach

✖ Bud Grant took over as head coach of the Vikings in 1967.

George Halas. But on September 17, 1961, the Vikings entered the NFL by dominating the Bears 37–13.

Van Brocklin had planned on the rookie Tarkenton to begin the season by watching and learning for a few weeks. However, he came off the bench against the Bears in relief of starter George Shaw and threw for 250 yards and four touchdowns. He quickly took over as the starter full time. It was not long before Tarkenton became one of the best quarterbacks in the league.

The rest of their first season didn't go quite as smoothly. The Vikings surrendered at least 28 points in nine of their final

13 games and allowed a whopping 407 points for the season. They finished 3–11. The Vikings allowed nearly 30 points per game in three of the next four seasons, too. They finally managed to put together a strong defensive season in 1964. It resulted in their first winning record at 8–5–1.

After the Vikings slid back to 7–7 in 1965 and 4–9–1 in 1966, Van Brocklin quit. He was replaced by Canadian Football League veteran coach Bud Grant, a former three-sport star at the University of Minnesota.

Meanwhile, Tarkenton was traded to the New York Giants for four high draft picks. The Vikings used the picks wisely, selecting future Pro Bowl offensive linemen Ron Yary and Ed White.

Grant worked wonders in Minnesota. With one game remaining in the 1968 season, the Vikings needed a win over the Philadelphia Eagles. They also needed Chicago to lose to Green Bay. If all that happened, they would earn their first playoff spot. The pressure became intense when the Vikings were informed that the Bears were losing.

Early in the second half, Minnesota linebacker Wally Hilgenberg forced a fumble. The Vikings recovered, and they began marching down the field.

Quarterback Joe Kapp led the Vikings to their first playoff appearance in 1968.

Minnesota cashed in when quarterback Joe Kapp tossed a go-ahead 30-yard touchdown pass to Gene Washington, and the Vikings went on to win 24–17. With the Bears' loss, the Vikings were heading to the playoffs.

The Vikings traveled to Baltimore to play the Colts. The Colts had been nearly unstoppable during the regular season. They had finished 13–1. Their hot streak continued in the playoffs. Baltimore beat the Vikings 24–14.

It was a disappointing loss for the Vikings. However, during that 1968 season the Vikings had shown that they were one of the league's elite teams. There would be many more playoff celebrations—and disappointments—to come.

CHAPTER 3

CAN'T WIN THE BIG ONE

The Purple People Eaters peaked in the early 1970s. Fresh off the Vikings' first Super Bowl appearance, they continued to make life miserable for opposing offenses. They surrendered fewer than 21 points in every regular-season game in 1970. They did it in all but one game in 1971.

Although the defense was strong, the offense simply did not have enough talent to win playoff games against superior competition. The Vikings lost in the first round of the playoffs in both 1970 and 1971. Including the Super Bowl IV loss against Kansas City in 1969, Minnesota scored a combined 33 points in three straight playoff games from the 1969 season to 1971. All of them were losses. The Vikings boasted an impressive regular-season mark of 35–7 during

Dolphins running back Larry Csonka carries two Vikings defenders into the end zone in Super Bowl VIII.

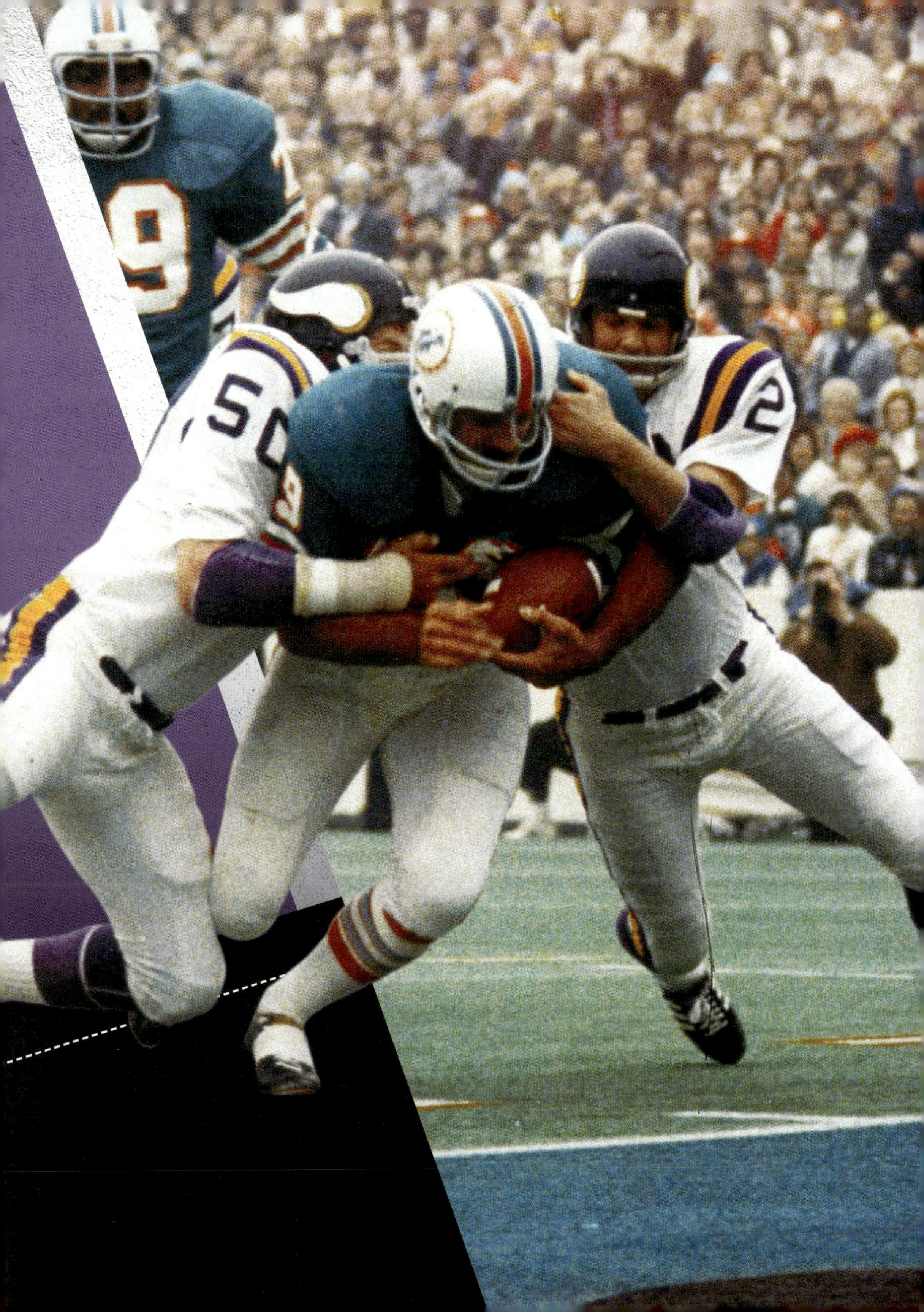

GROUND CHUCK

The Vikings selected Chuck Foreman in the first round of the 1973 NFL Draft. He made an immediate impact as a rookie, rushing for 801 yards and catching 37 passes. He was named the NFL Offensive Rookie of the Year in the process. In 1975 Foreman became the first Minnesota back to exceed 1,000 rushing yards, and he repeated the feat the next two years. He did more than run wild in 1975. Foreman also led the league with 73 receptions, scored 22 touchdowns, and earned All-Pro status for the only time in his career.

those three seasons. However, they had no title to show for it.

The Vikings needed more consistent play at quarterback. So they brought back an old friend. After five seasons with the New York Giants, Fran Tarkenton returned to Minnesota in 1972. He led the Vikings to the playoffs the next year. And this time, they began visiting the end zone more frequently.

Tarkenton threw for a combined 355 yards and three touchdowns in playoff victories over Washington and Dallas in 1973. First-year running back Chuck Foreman also contributed greatly in those wins for Minnesota. Those victories thrust the Vikings back into the Super Bowl against the Miami Dolphins. However, the offense again sputtered with a championship on the line. The Vikings lost 24–7 to the Dolphins in Super Bowl VIII.

✖ Vikings running back Chuck Foreman drags a Bills defender with him in 1975.

    A nearly identical scenario played out in 1974. The team waltzed into the playoffs with a 10–4 record. Minnesota beat the St. Louis Cardinals and the Los Angeles Rams to reach the Super Bowl. But the offense again abandoned the Vikings on

✗ Drew Pearson outmaneuvers the Vikings' Paul Krause (22) and Nate Wright (43) for a controversial touchdown catch in the Cowboys' 17–14 victory in the 1975 playoffs.

the game's biggest stage. They fell 16–6 to the Pittsburgh Steelers, an emerging NFL power, in Super Bowl IX. The Vikings were held to 119 yards, including just 17 on the ground, against the Steelers. Tarkenton threw three interceptions in the defeat.

Minnesota continued on the same path. The Vikings won 12 of 14 regular-season games in 1975. But they lost in controversial style to the underdog Dallas Cowboys 17–14 in the first round of the playoffs. Minnesota then went 11–2–1 in 1976. The Vikings performed well in that season's playoffs. They defeated Washington 35–20 and the Rams 24–13 to qualify for their fourth Super Bowl in eight seasons.

The Vikings' frustrations, however, reached a boiling point when they lost to the Oakland Raiders 32–14 in Super Bowl XI on January 9, 1977. After all, their defense had not given up that many points in a game in four seasons. The national media criticized their performance.

"The football game was essentially over [by halftime], as so many Super Bowls have been concluded prematurely by the Vikings, who somehow seem to save their worst for

DID DREW PUSH OFF?

One of the most controversial plays in Vikings history occurred in the NFC first-round playoff game against Dallas on December 28, 1975. The Vikings led 14–10 in the final minute when Cowboys quarterback Roger Staubach threw a 50-yard "Hail Mary" pass to wide receiver Drew Pearson for a touchdown. Vikings fans and players have claimed ever since that Pearson pushed Minnesota defensive back Nate Wright to help secure the catch. They say Pearson should have been called for offensive pass interference. Pearson has denied that contention. Dallas won 17–14.

LITTLE EMOTION, BIG WINNER

Bud Grant stood stoically on the sidelines when he coached the Vikings. He rarely cracked a smile or spoke with emotion to the media or his players after games. He shared authority with his assistant coaches. But he knew how to win.

Though Grant's teams lost four Super Bowls, they suffered through no losing seasons from 1968 to 1978. The Vikings qualified for the playoffs 10 times in those 11 years. Quarterback Fran Tarkenton spoke glowingly about his coach, with whom he enjoyed his best seasons.

"The players and coaches all knew who was in charge," said Tarkenton, who won the NFL MVP Award in 1975. "Bud let everyone do their job and respected them as a professional. It was an atmosphere ripe for individual and team success; everyone was motivated by his confidence in them."

[Super Bowl games]," wrote Dan Jenkins of *Sports Illustrated*. "The only fascinating part was how ingeniously easy Minnesota made it for the Oakland Raiders this time."

Through the 2018 season, the Vikings had not made it back to the Super Bowl. The Vikings team that lost to Oakland in Super Bowl XI was getting old. Linebacker Wally Hilgenberg, safety Paul Krause, Tarkenton, and all four Purple People Eaters would retire by 1979.

Oakland lineman Otis Sistrunk pursues Minnesota quarterback Fran Tarkenton in Super Bowl XI. The Vikings lost 32–14.

The Vikings lost to Dallas in the 1977 National Football Conference (NFC) Championship Game. Then they lost to Los Angeles in the first round in 1978. The Vikings combined for just 16 points in the two games. An era of greatness was over. The ultimate goal of winning a Super Bowl was not achieved. But more success was on the way. And so was one of the most stunning trades in NFL history.

CHAPTER 4

GOING GREEN

By the 1980s, the Purple People Eaters were gone and the fans were blue. The defense that had terrorized opponents for more than a decade had become quite ordinary. So had the entire team.

Even the head coach had changed—twice. Bud Grant retired in 1984 and was replaced by assistant Les Steckel. Grant then returned for one year in 1985 after the Vikings set team records by giving up 484 points and losing 13 games in the 1984 season under Steckel.

The next head coach was far more successful. Jerry Burns guided the Vikings into the playoffs after the 1987 season. The Vikings won on the road over the New Orleans Saints and the San Francisco 49ers to get to the NFC Championship

Herschel Walker holds up his new Minnesota jersey after he was acquired from Dallas in 1989.

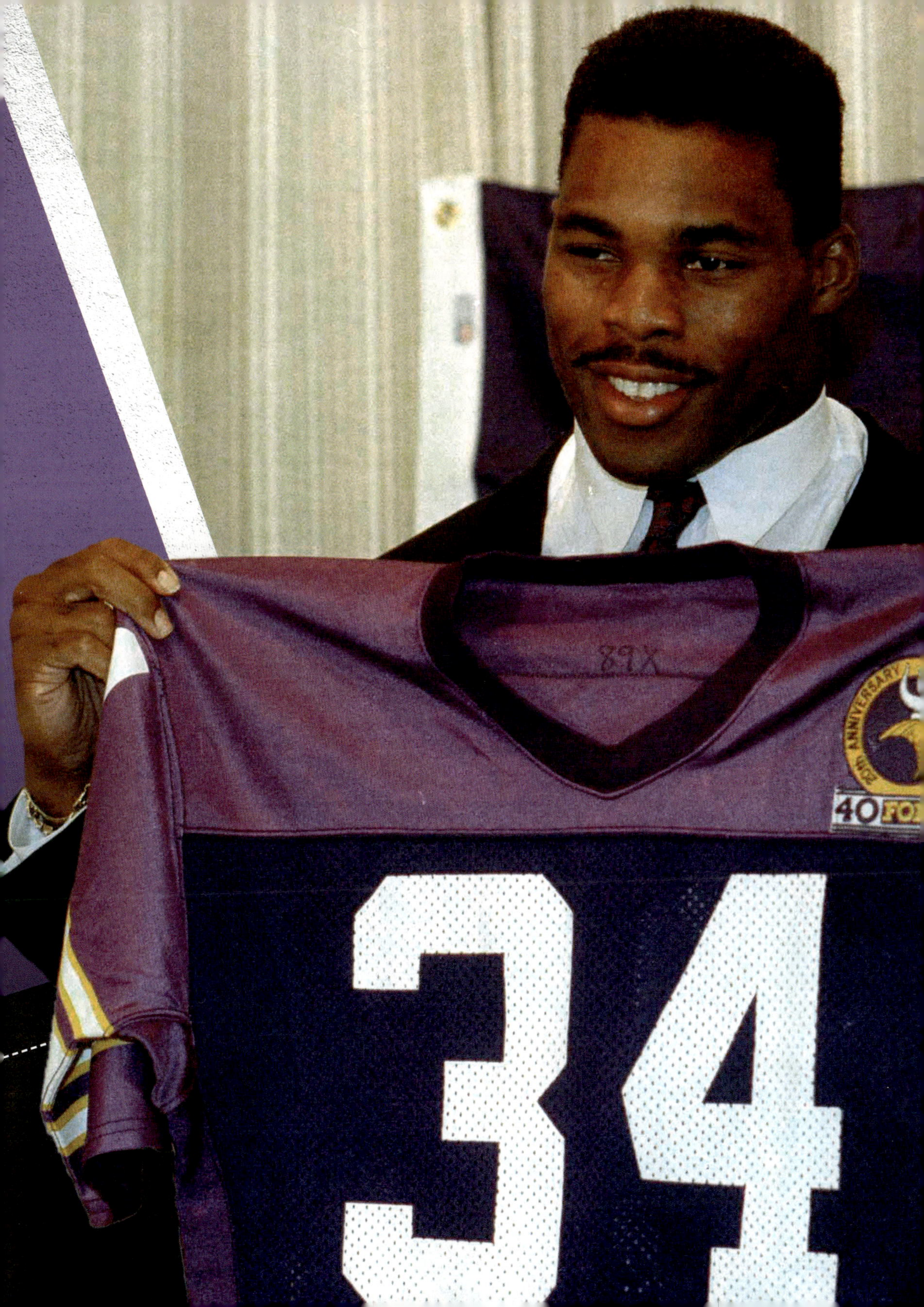
ANNIVERSARY
40
34

THE SACK MAN

Chris Doleman was a fixture at defensive end for the Vikings from 1985 to 1993. He also played for the team in 1999, his final NFL season. He was among the top tacklers in the league. He recorded more than 100 tackles in 1985 and 1991. But his finest attribute was as a pass rusher. Doleman led the NFL in sacks with 21.0 in 1989. He finished his career with 150.5. Through 2018, that ranked fifth in NFL history. Doleman racked up at least 10 sacks in eight seasons in his NFL career.

Game at Washington. However, a fifth Super Bowl berth was denied when the Vikings lost 17–10.

The Vikings returned to the playoffs again after the 1988 season. They advanced to the second round before falling to the powerful 49ers 34–9 in San Francisco.

The Vikings were in need of some new faces. Quarterback Wade Wilson did not produce statistics that amazed anyone. The running game was mediocre. Wide receiver Anthony Carter and tight end Steve Jordan were the Vikings' only receiving threats. Led by defensive end Chris Doleman, linebacker Scott Studwell, safety Joey Browner, and cornerback Carl Lee, the defense was strong. But it did not play at a Purple People Eaters–like level.

Vikings general manager Mike Lynn made a bold move to inject some life into the offense. He traded a package of

✕ Vikings receiver Anthony Carter eludes tacklers in Minnesota's 36–24 upset of the 49ers in San Francisco in January 1988.

players and draft picks to the Dallas Cowboys for running back Herschel Walker. However, the trade didn't work out. In fact, it turned out to be one of the most disastrous deals in NFL history.

Walker was a straight-ahead runner, making him a bad fit with the Vikings offense, which emphasized misdirection and short passes to versatile running backs. In two and a half seasons with the team, Walker rushed for 100 yards in a game

BAD DEAL OF THE CENTURY

Five games into the 1989 season, Vikings general manager Mike Lynn decided that one great running back was all that stood between his team and a Super Bowl championship. So he made one of the most significant and controversial trades in NFL history.

The Vikings acquired running back Herschel Walker from Dallas for five players and several draft picks. This included three picks in the first round and three in the second round. The football world was stunned.

The deal would become a disaster. Walker had rushed for 1,514 yards for the Cowboys in 1988. But he played just two and a half years with the Vikings and never gained 1,000 yards in a season. Minnesota compiled a 21–23 record with Walker and then released him.

just four times. Worse, the Vikings lost to the 49ers in their playoff opener in 1989 and didn't make the postseason the next two years.

Jerry Burns retired after the 1991 season. But rather than promote an assistant or hire a coach with NFL experience, they picked Dennis Green. He had turned around a struggling football program at Stanford University.

The positive effect was immediate. Green released a number of underperforming veterans, including Walker, Browner, and defensive tackle Keith Millard. The Vikings

✖ Dennis Green, shown in 1999, coached the Vikings from 1992 to 2001. The team made the playoffs eight times in his 10 seasons in charge.

sprinted to a 5–1 record to start the regular season. They were playing well on the field and enjoying themselves off it.

"He brought us a rebirth," defensive back Todd Scott said. "When you look at where we are, look at Dennis Green first. He's responsible for the change."

So was a new core of players. The disastrous trade for Walker cost Minnesota a number of draft choices. But the

29

GREAT GUARD

The Vikings have been fortunate to have some of the top offensive linemen in NFL history, including Ron Yary, Gary Zimmerman, and Mick Tingelhoff. But none performed better for a longer period than Randall McDaniel. McDaniel started 15 games as a rookie in 1988. He then began a run of 12 consecutive Pro Bowl seasons. During that time, he was named to nine All-Pro teams. He was enshrined in the Pro Football Hall of Fame in 2009.

Vikings still managed to add talent. They signed wide receiver Cris Carter in 1990. He had been released by the Eagles. Carter became one of the best at his position throughout the 1990s.

The Vikings picked running back Terry Allen in the ninth round of the 1991 draft. He quickly emerged as a cornerstone of the ground game. Allen rushed for 1,201 yards and 13 touchdowns in 1992.

Also, Randall McDaniel and Gary Zimmerman proved to be two of the best offensive linemen in the NFL for more than a decade. And a defensive line led by Doleman, Henry Thomas, and emerging star John Randle was racking up sacks.

Green guided the Vikings into the playoffs in eight of his first nine seasons. However, it seemed nothing had changed. Minnesota still played poorly in the postseason. The Vikings were eliminated in the first round after the 1992, 1993, 1994, and 1996 seasons. Green finally won his first playoff game with

✖ Rookie wide receiver Randy Moss, *right*, helped the 1998 Vikings set an NFL single-season record with 556 points.

a road upset of the New York Giants in December 1997 before being eliminated the next week at San Francisco.

In 1998, however, the Vikings appeared ready to take a trip to their fifth Super Bowl. An offense led by quarterback Randall Cunningham, running back Robert Smith, and wide receivers Cris Carter and rookie Randy Moss rolled over almost every defense it faced. The Vikings scored 556 points that season, an average of 34.8 per game. It remained the most points scored in a season by one team in NFL history until New England surpassed it in 2007. The Vikings finished the regular season 15–1 and entered the playoffs favored to win the Super Bowl.

Minnesota continued to dominate with a 41–21 win over the Arizona Cardinals in the first round of the playoffs. But in the NFC Championship Game, the defense let them down. Cunningham played well. But Minnesota allowed Atlanta Falcons quarterback Chris Chandler to throw for 340 yards and three touchdowns on the day.

"We had such tremendous expectations," said Vikings kicker Gary Anderson. "That makes it 10 times more disappointing."

Anderson had made all 35 field goals he had attempted during the regular season. But with a little less than three minutes left and the Vikings up by seven, Anderson missed a field goal that likely would have sealed the win. The 38-yard attempt sailed wide by about a foot. After the miss, Atlanta quickly seized the momentum. The Falcons drove down the field, and Chandler's 16-yard touchdown pass to Terance Mathis tied the game, forcing overtime.

And when Falcons kicker Morten Andersen booted a 38-yard field goal in overtime, the Vikings experienced a crushing defeat, 30–27.

More heartache soon followed. Things were shaping up nicely two seasons later for the Vikings. They went 11–5 to win the NFC Central. Led by second-year quarterback Daunte Culpepper, they easily beat the New Orleans Saints 34–16 in the divisional round of the playoffs. Then came the NFC Championship Game against the New York Giants. The Giants crushed the visiting Vikings 41–0. It was a loss that perhaps equaled the Super Bowl defeats in terms of humiliation.

The Vikings reached the playoffs after the 2004 and 2008 seasons but were eliminated by the Philadelphia Eagles both times. The team had hired head coach Brad Childress in 2006 to turn things around. By 2009 they were almost there.

TRAGEDY

The Vikings received a horrible emotional blow during training camp in 2001 when Pro Bowl offensive tackle Korey Stringer collapsed and died during a workout. Sweltering temperatures on that August day at Vikings training camp in Mankato, Minnesota, played a role in his death. Doctors said he died because of heat stroke. The heat index—a combination of temperature and humidity—had reached 110 degrees that morning.

CHAPTER 5

NEW ERA, SIMILAR RESULTS

The Vikings were in need of a boost before the 2009 season. The team had acquired many talented players who had guided the team to the 2008 playoffs. But many fans believed the team needed a star quarterback to get them over the hump. The team got that quarterback—one few Vikings fans ever could have imagined seeing in purple.

Brett Favre had played for the rival Green Bay Packers for 16 seasons before joining the New York Jets in 2008. Favre was a constant thorn in the Vikings' side while with the Packers. But Vikings fans gladly welcomed the legendary quarterback in 2009.

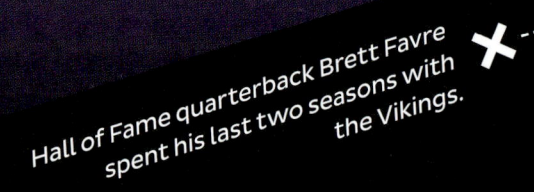

Hall of Fame quarterback Brett Favre spent his last two seasons with the Vikings.

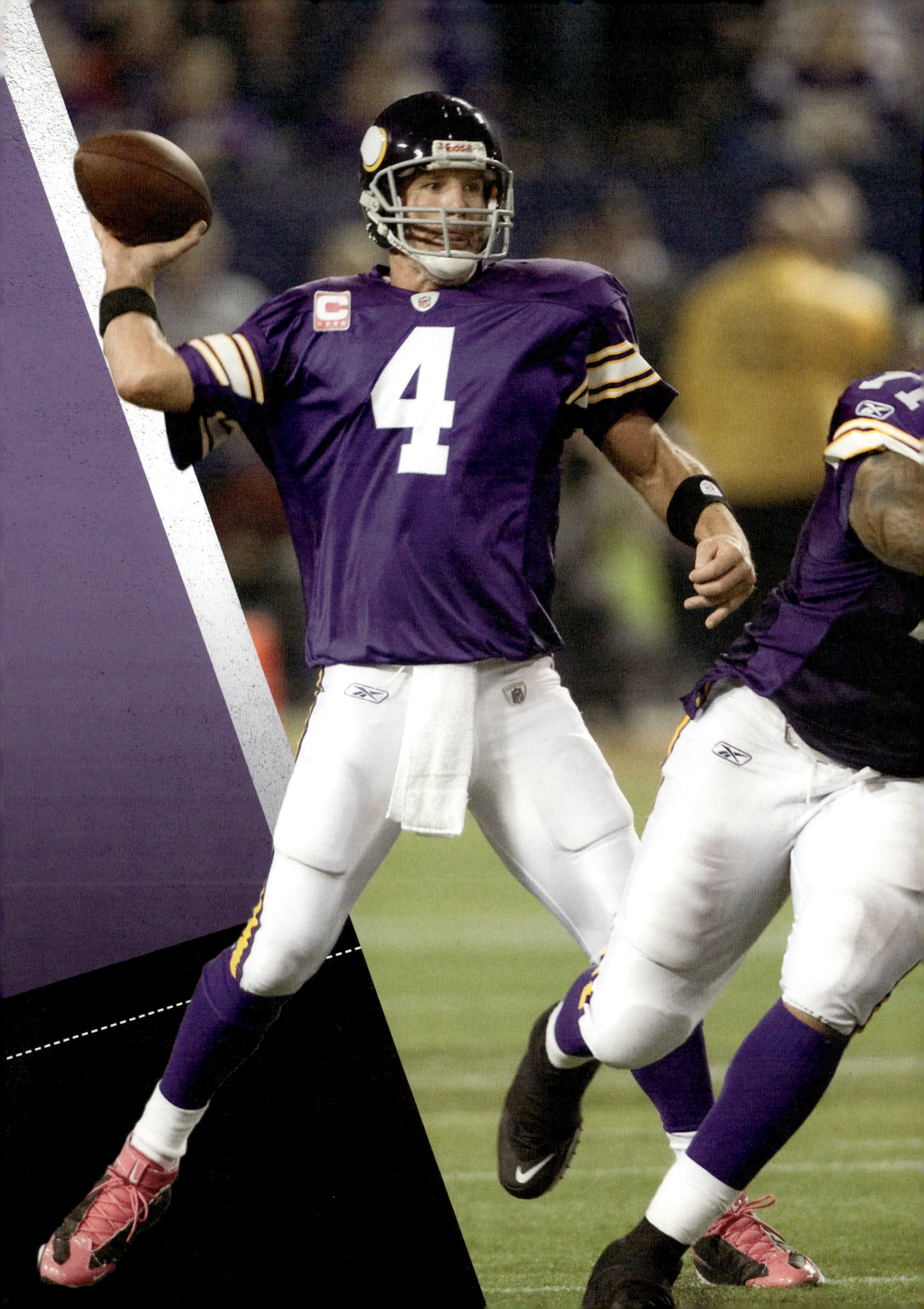

✗ Favre and running back Adrian Peterson provided the Vikings with a powerful one-two punch in 2009.

The Vikings rolled into the playoffs in 2009 behind Favre, running back Adrian Peterson, and defensive end Jared Allen. A fifth Super Bowl appearance again looked possible after a 34–3 drubbing of the Dallas Cowboys in the divisional round.

The Vikings and the New Orleans Saints had been the top teams in the NFC all season. They met in New Orleans in the NFC Championship Game. Minnesota played well all game but was plagued by turnovers. The Vikings lost three fumbles and Favre threw two interceptions. Still, the game was tied 28–28 late in the fourth quarter.

As time ran down, Favre drove the Vikings into field-goal range. However, a costly penalty pushed them back. Then New Orleans' Tracy Porter intercepted a Favre pass to end the threat. The Saints won 31–28 in overtime and then won the Super Bowl two weeks later.

When Favre agreed to play one more season, the Vikings expected to be Super Bowl contenders once again. Instead, almost everything went wrong. They finished 6–10. And Favre retired for good after the season.

Defensive coordinator Leslie Frazier replaced Childress midway through the 2010 season. He then became the

DOME COLLAPSE

The 2010 season was a disastrous one on and off the field for the Vikings. Just hours before they were supposed to play a home game on December 12 against the Giants, the roof of the Metrodome collapsed due to heavy snow. The team was forced to play a "home" game in Detroit at the home of the Lions. The Metrodome was still out of service a week later, so the Vikings played their first outdoor home game since 1981 at the University of Minnesota. The Vikings lost both games.

Undrafted wide receiver Adam Thielen emerged as one of the top players at his position in 2017.

permanent head coach for 2011. After a disastrous 3–13 season, the Vikings rebounded to make the playoffs in 2012.

They did so with the help of Peterson. He put together his best season, finishing just eight yards short of the all-time rushing record. He rushed for more than 100 yards in eight straight games. After the season, he was named NFL MVP.

But while the running game was effective, the Vikings struggled to find a quarterback. Second-year player Christian Ponder started all 16 games in 2012. But his poor play in 2013 forced the team to try veterans Josh Freeman and Matt Cassel. In 2014, it was Ponder, Cassel, and rookie Teddy Bridgewater.

Bridgewater played well enough to give fans hope for the future. He won the starting job in 2015 and led the Vikings to an 11–5 record. Bridgewater was a good passer, but also could use his legs to run and escape pressure.

The Vikings' history of heartbreak resurfaced in the playoffs. They faced the Seattle Seahawks at TCF Bank Stadium on the campus of the University of Minnesota. That was their temporary home while a new stadium was being built. On a very cold day, both offenses struggled. The Vikings led most of the game but trailed 10–9 late. Kicker Blair Walsh attempted a 27-yard field goal with 20 seconds left to win the game. But he missed.

The Vikings opened U.S. Bank Stadium in Minneapolis in 2016. It was an exciting new era of Vikings football. But the season did not get off to a good start when Bridgewater was injured in training camp. He suffered a serious knee injury that almost ended his career. To replace him, the team traded for veteran Sam Bradford, who'd had previous success in the NFL with the Philadelphia Eagles. But Peterson missed most of the year with an injury and left the team after the season. The Vikings finished 8–8 and missed the playoffs.

Bradford was expected to be the starter in 2017. But quarterback woes struck again, or at least it looked that way, when Bradford got hurt. Then veteran backup Case Keenum came in and had an outstanding season, throwing 22 touchdown passes and only seven interceptions while averaging almost 250 passing yards per game in 15 games.

After going 13–3, the Vikings faced their old friends the Saints at home in the playoffs. Minnesota built a lead, but Drew Brees and the Saints made a big comeback to take the lead. Trailing 24–23 with 10 seconds left, Keenum threw a deep pass to Stefon Diggs on the right sideline. A Saints defender ducked his head to tackle Diggs but missed him completely. With no one between him and the goal line, Diggs ran the last 35 yards for a touchdown. The play became known as "the Minneapolis Miracle." But the Vikings had another disappointing effort in the NFC Championship Game, losing 38–7 at Philadelphia.

Rather than give Keenum another chance, the Vikings changed quarterbacks yet again for 2018, signing Kirk Cousins

Stefon Diggs scores the game-winning touchdown against New Orleans in January 2018 on a play known as "the Minneapolis Miracle."

from Washington. Cousins had great receivers to work with in Diggs and Adam Thielen. Thielen attended a Division II college in southern Minnesota and went unnoticed by NFL scouts. But by 2018, he had become one of the best receivers in the NFL. He opened the 2018 season with 100 yards or more in his first eight games, a new NFL record. However, the offense sputtered and the Vikings missed the playoffs with an 8–7–1 record.

Minnesota has had many great players in its history. So far that has not been enough to win a Super Bowl. Vikings fans hoped that their team had finally put together a core that could take them all the way.

TIMELINE

1960 — The NFL grants the twin cities of Minneapolis and St. Paul a franchise on January 28.

1961 — On September 17 the Vikings stun the Chicago Bears 37–13 in their first regular-season game at Metropolitan Stadium.

1967 — Norm Van Brocklin resigns as coach in February after a 4–9–1 season in 1966. Bud Grant takes the reins.

1968 — The Vikings earn their first division title and playoff spot with a 24–17 defeat of Philadelphia and a loss by Chicago on December 15.

1969 — The Vikings go 12–2 in the regular season, the best record in the NFL.

1970 — Minnesota defeats Cleveland on January 4 to reach Super Bowl IV, where Kansas City pulls off a 23–7 upset on January 11.

1974 — The Vikings lose in their second Super Bowl, 24–7 to Miami on January 13.

1975 — For the second straight year the Vikings lose in the Super Bowl, falling to Pittsburgh 16–6 on January 12.

1977 — The Vikings lose their fourth Super Bowl game in eight years with a 32–14 defeat to Oakland on January 9.

1982 — The Vikings open the Metrodome with a 17–10 win over Tampa Bay on September 12.

1984 — Grant retires and the Vikings go 3–13 under first-year head coach Les Steckel, prompting Grant to return for one more season.

1988 — Reaching the NFC title game for the first time since 1977, the Vikings fall 17–10 to Washington on January 17.

1989 — The Vikings make an ill-fated trade with Dallas for running back Herschel Walker, swapping six early draft choices in the process.

1992 — Dennis Green is hired as coach on January 10, setting off an era of excellence for the Vikings.

1999 — The 15–1 Vikings lose 30–27 to Atlanta in overtime in the NFC Championship Game on January 17.

2001 — Green leads the Vikings to another NFC title game, where they lose 41–0 to the New York Giants on January 14.

2010 — Quarterback Brett Favre leads the Vikings back to the NFC title game. But the Vikings turn the ball over five times in a 31–28 overtime loss to New Orleans on January 24.

2012 — NFL MVP Adrian Peterson rushes for 2,097 yards, just eight short of the single-season NFL record.

2018 — Following "the Minneapolis Miracle," the Vikings make the NFC Championship game but lose 38–7 at Philadelphia on January 21.

2019 — Quarterback Kirk Cousins arrives via free agency but the Vikings go 8–7–1 and fail to make the playoffs.

QUICK STATS

FRANCHISE HISTORY

1961–

SUPER BOWLS
(wins in bold)

1969 (IV), 1973 (VIII), 1974 (IX), 1976 (XI)

NFL CHAMPIONSHIP GAMES *(1961–69, wins in bold)*

1969

NFC CHAMPIONSHIP GAMES *(since 1970 AFL-NFL merger)*

1973, 1974, 1976, 1977, 1987, 1998, 2000, 2009, 2017

KEY COACHES

Bud Grant (1967–83, 1985): 158–96–5, 10–12 (playoffs)
Dennis Green (1992–2001): 97–62, 4–8 (playoffs)

KEY PLAYERS
(position, seasons with team)

Cris Carter (WR, 1990–2001)
Chris Doleman (DE, 1985–93, 1999)
Carl Eller (DE, 1964–78)
Chuck Foreman (RB, 1973–79)
Paul Krause (S, 1968–79)
Jim Marshall (DE, 1961–79)
Randall McDaniel (G, 1988–99)
Randy Moss (WR, 1998–2004)
Alan Page (DT, 1967–78)
Adrian Peterson (RB, 2007–16)
John Randle (DT, 1990–2000)
Harrison Smith (S, 2012–)
Robert Smith (RB, 1993–2000)
Fran Tarkenton (QB, 1961–66, 1972–78)
Mick Tingelhoff (C, 1962–78)
Ron Yary (OT, 1968–81)
Gary Zimmerman (OT, 1986–92)

HOME FIELDS

U.S. Bank Stadium (2016–)
TCF Bank Stadium (2014–15)
Hubert H. Humphrey Metrodome (1982–2013)
Metropolitan Stadium (1961–81)

* All statistics through 2018 season

QUOTES AND ANECDOTES

In the 1970s, the Vikings twice threatened to become the second team in NFL history to complete a regular season unbeaten. They fell short both times. Miami achieved that rare feat in 1972, and then finished the job by becoming the only team to ever remain undefeated through the playoffs and the Super Bowl. The Vikings won their first nine games in 1973 before they fell to Atlanta. They sprinted out to a 10–0 record in 1975 before they lost to Washington. They did win all their home games in both those seasons, however. In 1998 the Vikings finished with a franchise-best 15–1 record. Their one loss that season came in their eighth game, 27–24 at Tampa Bay.

NFL punters and place kickers of the late 1970s and early 1980s had to be a bit nervous when they saw Vikings linebacker Matt Blair across the field waiting for the ball to be snapped. Blair was a standout player. Through 2018 he ranked second in franchise history with 1,452 tackles. He earned six trips to the Pro Bowl. But his specialty was blocking kicks. He recorded a franchise-record 20.5 blocks during his career.

Pro Football Hall of Fame quarterback Warren Moon played three seasons with the Vikings after a standout tenure with the Houston Oilers. He threw for 8,492 yards and 51 touchdowns in his first two years with Minnesota and earned trips to the Pro Bowl in 1994 and 1995.

Bud Grant was known for his toughness on the sidelines. In 2016, at the age of 88, Grant showed he was as tough as ever. He was asked to toss the coin for the Vikings-Seahawks playoff game outdoors in Minneapolis. It was the third-coldest game in NFL history. Temperature at kickoff was minus-6 degrees Fahrenheit (minus-21°C). Grant strode out to midfield for the ceremonial coin toss in a short-sleeve shirt, apparently impervious to the cold.

GLOSSARY

coordinator
An assistant coach who is in charge of the offense or defense.

draft
A system that allows teams to acquire new players coming into a league.

franchise
A sports organization, including the top-level team and all minor league affiliates.

momentum
The sense that a team is playing well and will be difficult to stop.

Pro Bowl
The NFL's all-star game, in which the best players in the league compete.

rookie
A professional athlete in his or her first year of competition.

secondary
The defensive players—cornerbacks and safeties—who start the play farthest from the line.

veteran
A player who has played many years.

MORE INFORMATION

BOOKS

Campbell, Dave. *Minnesota Vikings*. Minneapolis, MN: Abdo Publishing, 2017.

Jacobson, Ryan and Lindsay VonRuden. *Adam Thielen: From Small Town to Football Star*. Minneapolis, MN: Lake 7 Creative, 2018.

Karras, Steven M. *Minnesota Vikings*. New York: AV2 by Weigl, 2018.

ONLINE RESOURCES

Booklinks
NONFICTION NETWORK
FREE! ONLINE NONFICTION RESOURCES

To learn more about the Minnesota Vikings, visit **abdobooklinks.com** or scan this QR code. These links are routinely monitored and updated to provide the most current information available.

PLACE TO VISIT

TCO Performance Center
2600 Vikings Circle
Eagan, MN 55121
952–828–6500
vikings.com/news/tco-performance-center

Opened in 2018, TCO Performance Center is the Vikings team headquarters and site of training camp. When not in use by the Vikings, it also has a small stadium for high school football games.

INDEX

Alderman, Grady, 12
Allen, Jared, 36
Allen, Terry, 30
Anderson, Gary, 32

Bradford, Sam, 40
Bridgewater, Teddy, 39
Browner, Joey, 26, 28
Burns, Jerry, 24, 28

Carter, Anthony, 26
Carter, Cris, 30, 32
Cassel, Matt, 39
Childress, Brad, 33, 37
Cousins, Kirk, 40–41
Culpepper, Daunte, 33
Cunningham, Randall, 31–32

Diggs, Stefon, 40–41
Doleman, Chris, 26, 30

Eller, Carl, 4

Favre, Brett, 34–37
Foreman, Chuck, 18
Frazier, Leslie, 37–38
Freeman, Josh, 39

Grant, Bud, 14, 22, 24
Green, Dennis, 28–31

Hilgenberg, Wally, 14, 22

Jordan, Steve, 26

Kapp, Joe, 7–9, 15
Krause, Paul, 8, 22

Larsen, Gary, 4
Lee, Carl, 26

Marshall, Jim, 4
Mason, Tommy, 12
McDaniel, Randall, 30
McElhenny, Hugh, 12
Millard, Keith, 28
Moss, Randy, 32

Osborn, Dave, 7, 8

Page, Alan, 4, 6
Peterson, Adrian, 36, 38, 40
Ponder, Christian, 39

Randle, John, 30
Reichow, Jerry, 12

Rose, Bert, 10

Scott, Todd, 29
Shaw, George, 13
Smith, Robert, 31
Steckel, Les, 24
Stringer, Korey, 33
Studwell, Scott, 26

Tarkenton, Fran, 12–14, 18, 20, 22
Thielen, Adam, 41
Thomas, Henry, 30
Tingelhoff, Mick, 12, 30

Van Brocklin, Norm, 10, 12, 13–14

Walker, Herschel, 27–29
Walsh, Blair, 39
Washington, Gene, 7, 15
White, Ed, 14
Wilson, Wade, 26
Winter, Max, 10
Wright, Nate, 21

Yary, Ron, 14, 30

Zimmerman, Gary, 30

ABOUT THE AUTHOR

Todd Ryan is a library assistant from the Upper Peninsula of Michigan. He lives near Houghton with his two cats, Izzo and Mooch.